ARTIFICIAL INTELLIGENCE
AND ENTERTAINMENT

BY TAMMY ENZ

raintree

a Capstone company — publishers for children

Raintree is an imprint of Capstone Global Library Limited, a company incorporated in England and Wales having its registered office at 264 Banbury Road, Oxford, OX2 7DY – Registered company number: 6695582

www.raintree.co.uk
myorders@raintree.co.uk

Edited by Karen Aleo and Christopher Harbo
Designed by Brann Garvey
Original illustrations © Capstone Global Library Limited 2020
Picture research by Pam Mitsakos and Tracy Cummins
Production by Kathy McColley
Originated by Capstone Global Library Ltd
Printed and bound in India

ISBN 978 1 4747 8181 7 (hardcover)   ISBN 978 1 4747 7107 8 (paperback)
23 22 21 20 19   23 22 21 20 19
10 9 8 7 6 5 4 3 2 1   10 9 8 7 6 5 4 3 2 1

British Library Cataloguing in Publication Data
A full catalogue record for this book is available from the British Library.

Acknowledgements
We would like to thank the following for permission to reproduce photographs: Alamy: age fotostock, 22-23; AP Photo: Seth Wenig, 10; Getty Images: Anadolu Agency/Salih Zeki Fazlioglu, 26-27 (top), Bloomberg/Yuriko Nakao, 25, Yvonne Hemsey, 7; iStockphoto: mphillips007, 20-21; Newscom/MCT/ Handout, 16-17, YNA/Yonhap News, 12-13 (top); Shutterstock: Action Sports Photography, 24, Andrey Suslov, 28-29, Brian Kienzle, 12 (bottom left), EpicStockMedia, 26 (bottom middle), ESB Professional, 14-15, ImageFlo, 4-5, khoamartin, 19, Mark Nazh, Cover, MS711, 18, Supphachai Salaeman, Design Element; The Image Works: ©dpa/ullstein bild, 8-9. The publisher does not endorse products whose logos may appear on objects in images in this book.

Every effort has been made to contact copyright holders of material reproduced in this book. Any omissions will be rectified in subsequent printings if notice is given to the publisher.

All the internet addresses (URLs) given in this book were valid at the time of going to press. However, due to the dynamic nature of the internet, some addresses may have changed, or sites may have changed or ceased to exist since publication. While the author and publisher regret any inconvenience this may cause readers, no responsibility for any such changes can be accepted by either the author or the publisher.

CONTENTS

INTRODUCTION

AI AND ENTERTAINMENT

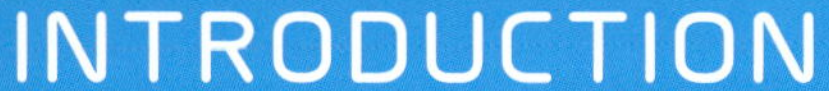

You are standing in your bedroom, but you're in the middle of a war zone. Laser beams fly over your head. Explosions spew dirt into the air. Suddenly your favourite video game character pops out from under the bed. You try to dodge its blasts, but the character guesses your move. Game over!

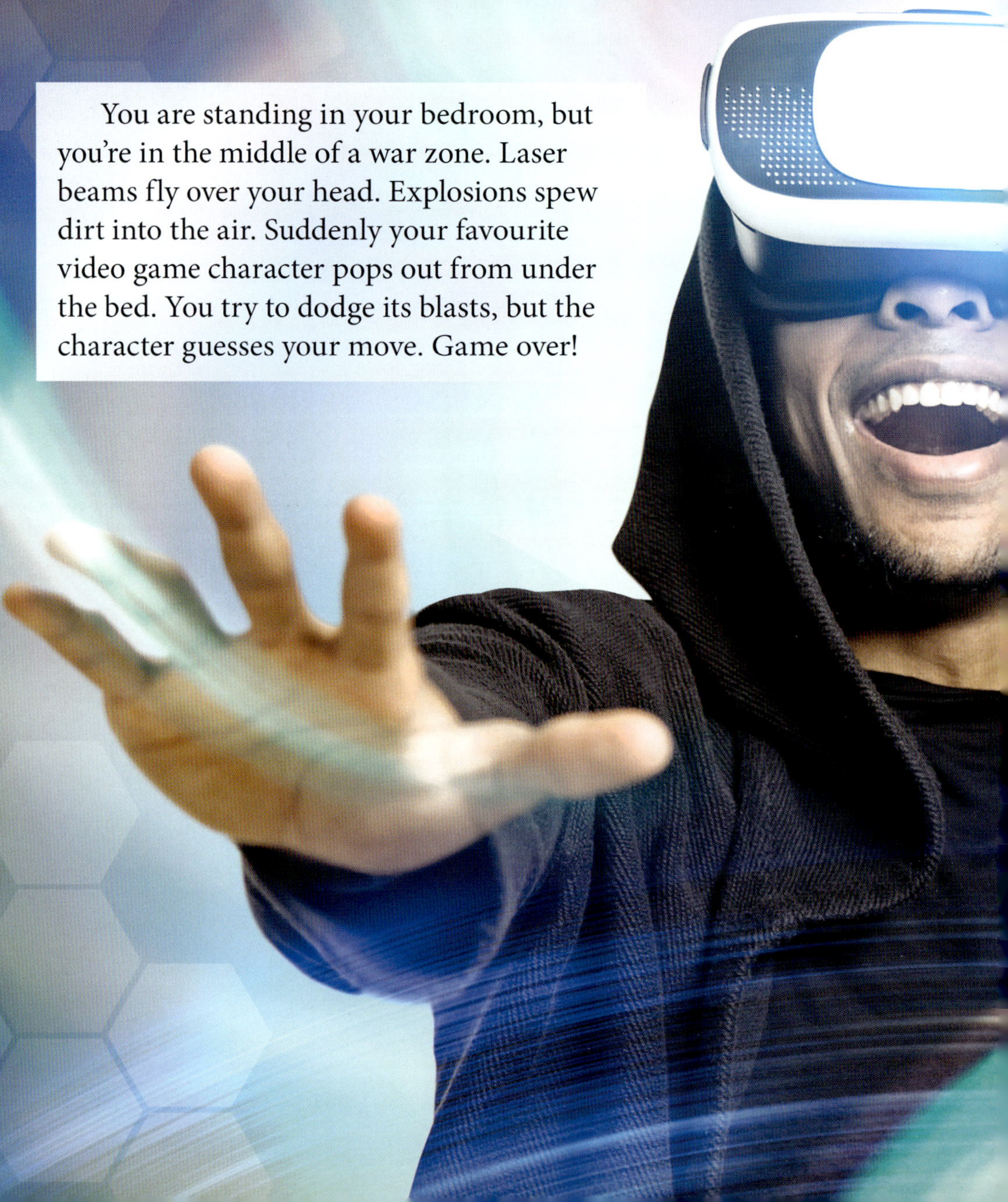

You pull off your **augmented reality** (AR) glasses and flop down on your bed. A robot rolls up next to you. It knows you're sad because you lost the game. It starts playing your favourite song to cheer you up. It then snaps a photo of your frowning face, which makes you laugh.

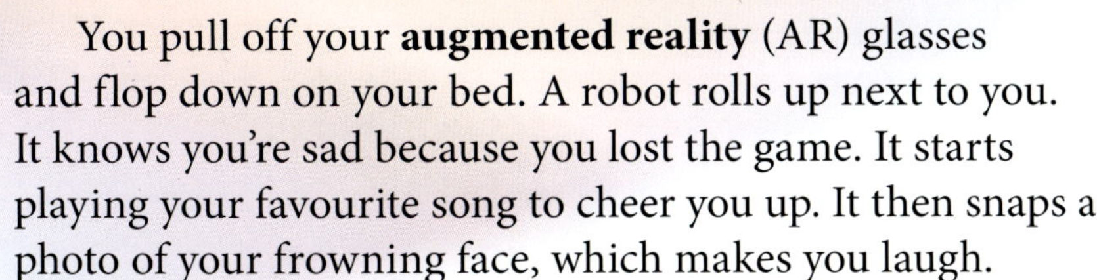

Does this scene sound as if it's from a futuristic film or TV programme? It's not. This reality is closer than you think. The world of entertainment is already changing because of artificial intelligence (AI) – and it's about to explode!

augmented reality computer-generated world created over the real world

EARLY AI

Artificial intelligence is the ability of machines to solve problems and perform tasks that would normally require human intelligence. One part of AI is known as **machine learning**. A machine learns by taking in large amounts of data and analysing it. Then it **predicts** what will happen next based on the information it has received. The more information AI analyses, the better the machine's predictions become.

DEEP BLUE

Many people first saw AI in action in 1996. Millions watched a six-game chess match. One player was the world chess champion, Garry Kasparov. The other player was a supercomputer called Deep Blue created by the International Business Machines Corporation (IBM).

machine learning way a computer learns

predict say what you think will happen in the future

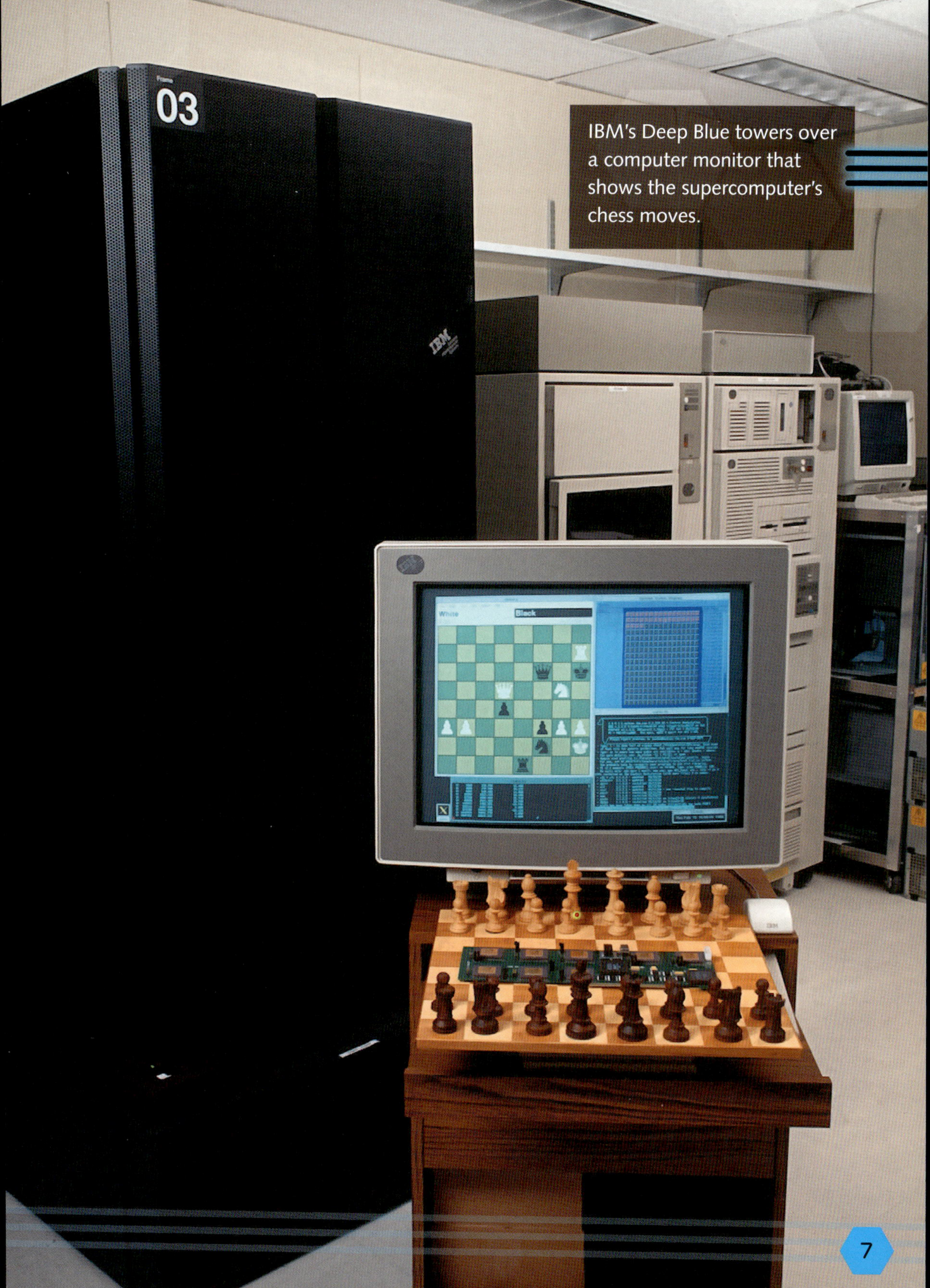

IBM's Deep Blue towers over a computer monitor that shows the supercomputer's chess moves.

World chess champion Garry Kasparov squares off against Deep Blue during their first match-up in 1996.

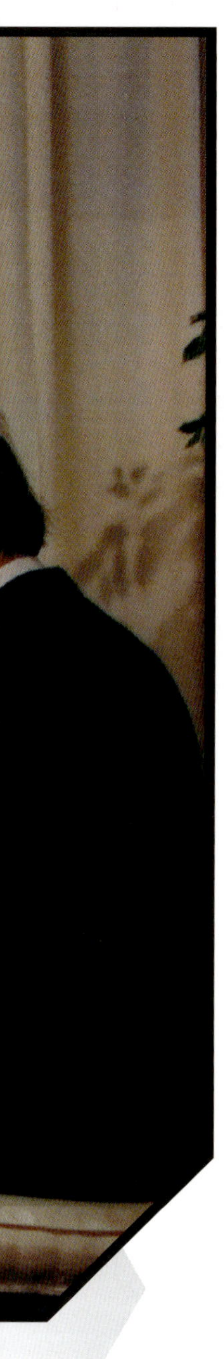

This was not the first match between Kasparov and Deep Blue. They had played each other one year earlier. Kasparov won that match four games to two. But now Deep Blue had received many upgrades and its engineers were hungry for a rematch.

The 1997 rematch started well for Kasparov. He won the first game. But Deep Blue came back with a win in game two. Then the next three games ended in a tie. Kasparov really began feeling the pressure going into the sixth game. In fewer than 20 moves, he lost the final game, and the match, to the computer program. Deep Blue had used AI to out-think a human.

How did Deep Blue pull off the win? Chess experts helped program its **software**. They gave Deep Blue the coding for different chess moves. With this data, Deep Blue used **strategy** and **logic** to win the game.

FACT

Deep Blue could analyse more than 200 million possible chess positions per second.

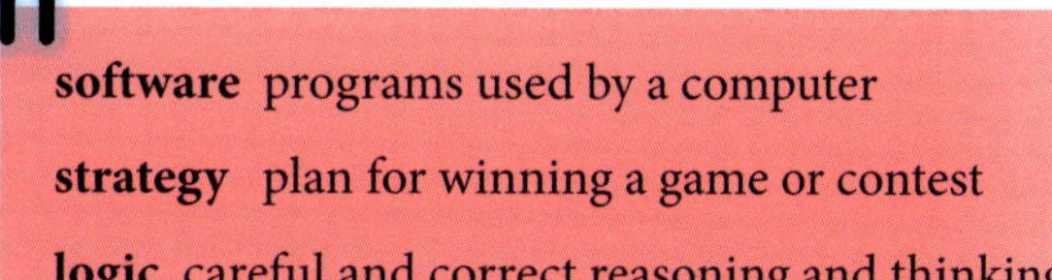

software programs used by a computer

strategy plan for winning a game or contest

logic careful and correct reasoning and thinking

WATSON PLAYS *JEOPARDY*

In the years following Deep Blue's win, computers became even more advanced. They could process huge amounts of data very quickly. By the mid-2000s, computer engineers at IBM were ready to test AI in a different game. They set their sights on *Jeopardy*.

Former champion Ken Jennings prepares to face IBM's Watson on *Jeopardy* in 2011.

Jeopardy is a TV **trivia** game show in which players must understand language. Players are first given an answer, and then they must provide the question that goes with it. For instance, a player might be given this answer: "He lost his chess match to Deep Blue in 1997." Then the player must provide the question: "Who is Garry Kasparov?"

For a machine to play *Jeopardy*, it would need to learn a lot of trivia. It would also need to understand phrases. And it would need to work backwards from an answer to create the question.

DOCTOR WATSON

IBM continued to improve Watson and shrink its size. Now the supercomputer is helping doctors plan cancer treatments. It **scans** through medical journals. It looks at thousands of cases and studies a patient's needs. Then it comes up with a treatment plan. Soon Watson will help doctors to treat other diseases too.

To tackle these AI challenges, IBM created Watson. This supercomputer took years to design and was the size of a large bedroom. To prepare for *Jeopardy*, engineers programmed it with 200 million pages of information. Then it challenged two of *Jeopardy*'s most successful champions in 2011. The competition was fierce, but in the end Watson easily beat both humans.

trivia general knowledge facts

scan look at closely and carefully

SELF-TAUGHT ALPHAGO

A company called DeepMind soon followed Watson's success. DeepMind's goal is to use machine learning to solve problems. In 2014 it began work on AlphaGo. This computer program used AI to learn the ancient board game Go.

Go is played on a square grid with black and white stones. The goal is to try to surround and capture an **opponent's** stones. The game's rules are simple. But the possible moves are endless – which makes the game very difficult for a machine to learn. But DeepMind faced the challenge. It showed AlphaGo thousands of human Go matches to understand the game. It also made AlphaGo play the game against different copies of itself to become a better player. DeepMind's efforts paid off. In March 2016, AlphaGo beat master Go player Lee Sedol four games to one.

After AlphaGo's success, DeepMind took machine learning to the next level with AlphaGo Zero. This **enhanced** AI program didn't need to watch human Go matches at all. AlphaGo Zero learned by just playing Go against itself. In 2017, AlphaGo Zero beat the original AlphaGo 100 games to none!

FACT

AlphaGo Zero was not programmed specifically for Go. It can be used to help solve problems in many areas. For example, it can help scientists to develop new medicines.

Go master Lee Sedol makes a move against AlphaGo in a 2016 match.

opponent person who competes against another person

enhanced made better or greater

CHAPTER 2

AI IN VIDEO GAMES

You may not have played against AlphaGo or Watson, but you've probably seen artificial intelligence in video games. Many video games use AI to learn your style of play. AI allows the game's characters to adjust to your actions. For example, over time AI learns your combat patterns, or how you fight. Then it creates enemies that can predict your moves. The better AI becomes at predicting your actions, the more challenging the game becomes.

But would human players stand a chance against a fully AI-operated game? Because AI can think and react faster than humans, it can easily win. In real-time games such as *WarCraft*, game designers had to simplify AI to improve a player's odds. Many designers want to limit the role of AI in video games so people still have a chance to win.

FACT

The video game *Petz* was one of the first AI games. AI allowed **digital** pets to be trained based on the player's style of play.

AI makes video games more unpredictable and challenging.

digital involving or relating to the use of computers

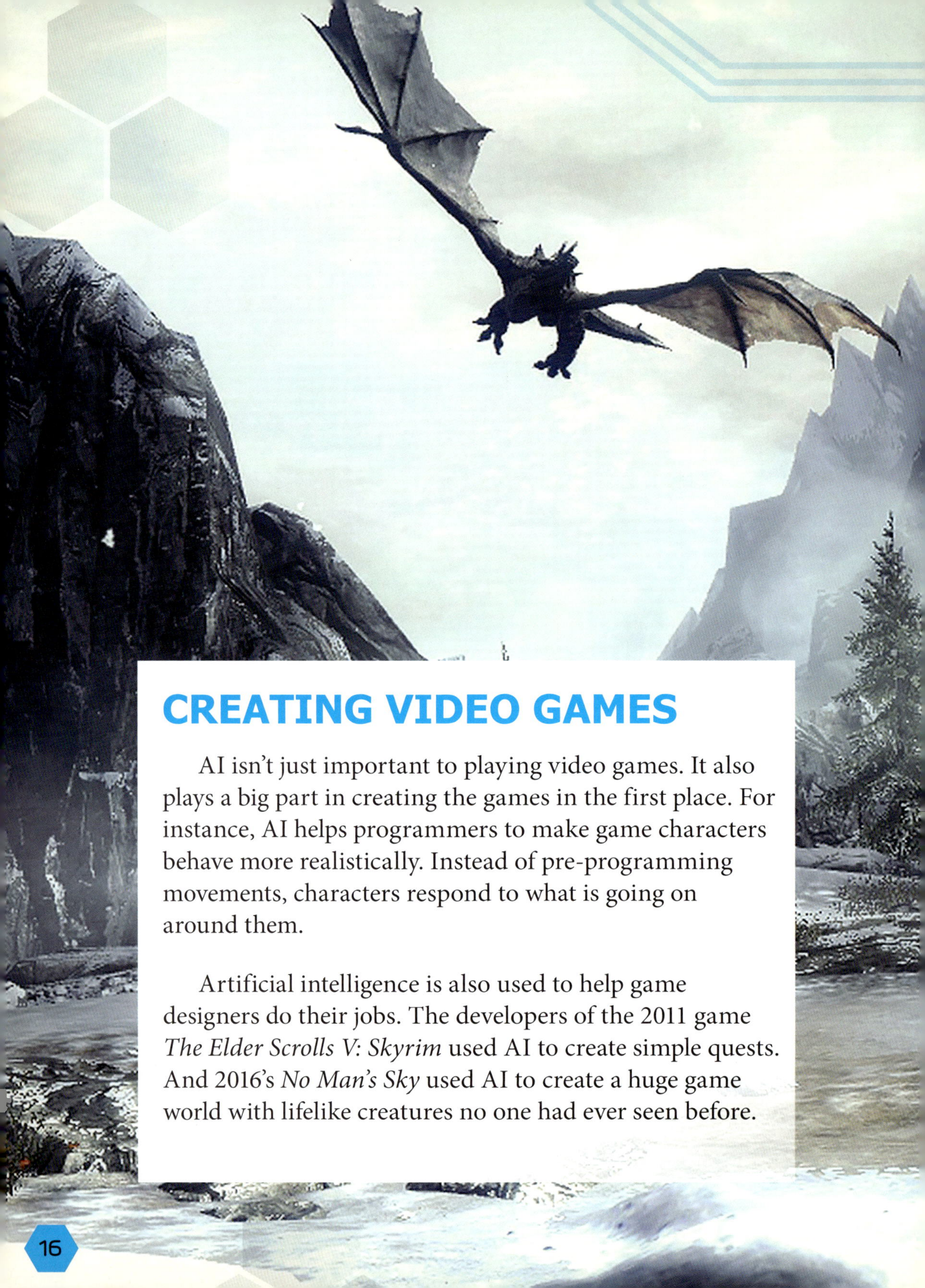

CREATING VIDEO GAMES

AI isn't just important to playing video games. It also plays a big part in creating the games in the first place. For instance, AI helps programmers to make game characters behave more realistically. Instead of pre-programming movements, characters respond to what is going on around them.

Artificial intelligence is also used to help game designers do their jobs. The developers of the 2011 game *The Elder Scrolls V: Skyrim* used AI to create simple quests. And 2016's *No Man's Sky* used AI to create a huge game world with lifelike creatures no one had ever seen before.

AI may one day even create all new games from scratch. Researcher Michael Cook's Angelina program thinks up games that no one has thought of before. It finds images on the internet and uses them to create interesting backgrounds. Angelina also uses social media and news stories to come up with game ideas. It then develops rules to go along with them.

The Elder Scrolls V: Skyrim also used AI to allow non-player characters to behave according to what was happening around them.

AUGMENTED REALITY AND VIRTUAL REALITY GAMES

Artificial intelligence is a must in creating augmented reality (AR) and **virtual reality** (VR) games. AR games blend the digital world with the real world. People use special glasses or other digital devices to see the game come alive in a real space. Characters can appear to bounce across the floor and do other things in the room. For example, *Minecraft* characters might jump up on your coffee table.

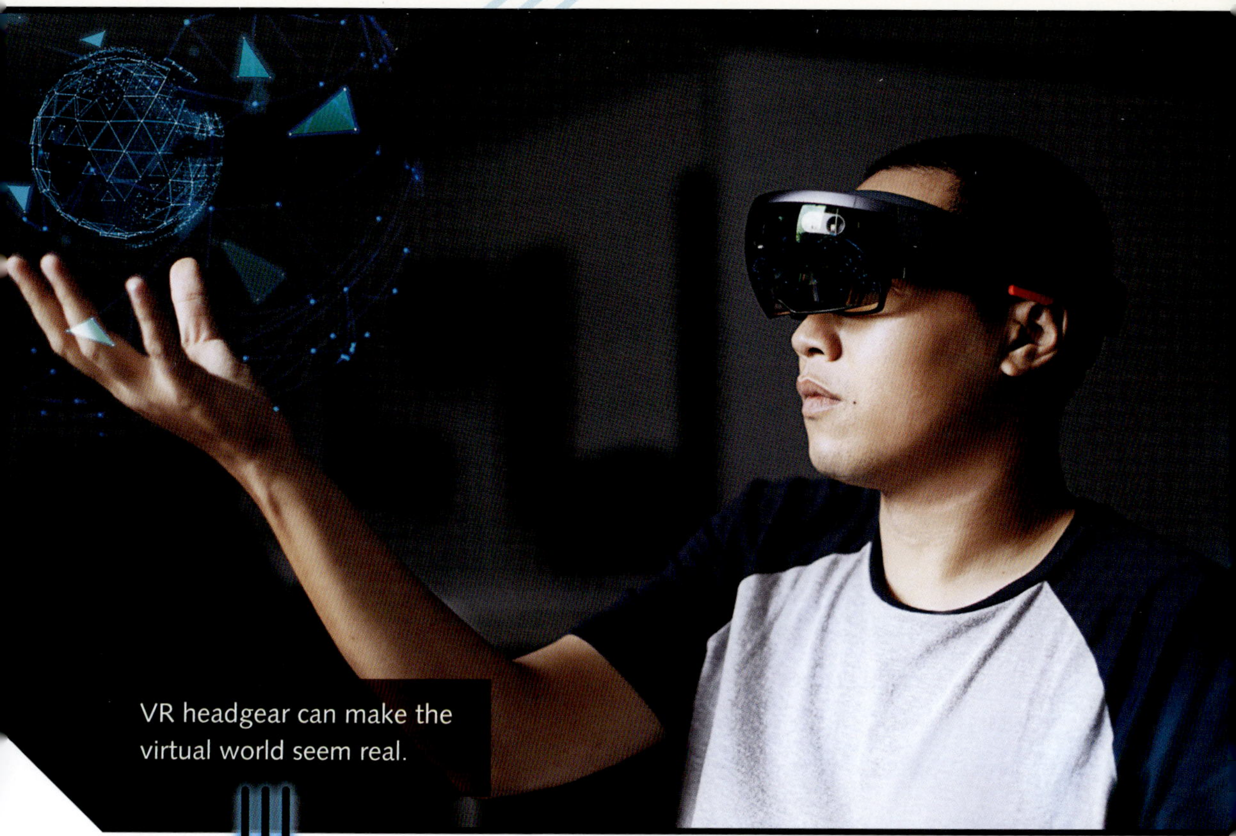

VR headgear can make the
virtual world seem real.

AI plays an important part in making AR games work.
It focuses on the objects in a room. AI allows the game
to learn where the walls, floors and furniture are placed.
It then puts game characters in the space. Each time the
game is played in a new room, it is a new experience.

Virtual reality takes gaming to another level. VR
uses headgear to make you feel as if you're actually inside
the game, and you can play games in 3D. Combining AI
with VR adds to the fun. It allows you to **interact** with
AI-controlled characters in a virtual world.

virtual reality computer-generated 3D world
with which humans can interact

interact action between people, groups or things

CHAPTER 3

AI FOR MUSIC, FILMS AND MORE

Gaming isn't the only type of entertainment that uses AI. Digital assistants such as Siri, Alexa, Cortana and Google Assistant use AI to help you find music or films. Do you know only a few words from a song? Tell them to a digital assistant, and it can find and play the song. These programs can also suggest other songs you might like based on what you usually listen to.

ROBOT ASSISTANT

A robot called Zenbo has been designed to entertain you much like a digital assistant. But instead of just a "voice", this AI robot follows you around the house! It can play music or videos and read you stories. Zenbo even recognizes your face. It can also take photos and videos of you to record your life.

Services such as Netflix make TV programme and film suggestions based on your likes too. They use AI to suggest things that are similar to what you've already watched. Netflix also discovers what people like by what they've watched several times.

FACT

Eighty per cent of everything watched on Netflix is discovered with the help of AI recommendations.

AI AND FILMS

AI not only helps to make video games, but also films. One key area AI helps film-makers with is large crowd scenes. In the early 2000s, the AI software Massive was developed for The Lord of the Rings trilogy. It created huge armies in which opposing characters could fight against each other. Since then, Massive has been used on several films for similar crowd scenes.

Computer-generated characters are common in today's films. With the help of motion capture systems, film-makers can make digital characters, such as monsters and aliens, that act and move in natural ways. But creating believable digital humans is still hard to do. Our eyes and brains are very good at picking out details that don't look quite right. But the use of AI is starting to fool us. It studies human movements, expressions and voices to create digital humans that look completely real.

FACT

AI has also been used to help make film trailers. It scans hundreds of scenes from a film. Then it pulls out the most exciting or scary shots to include in a trailer.

Motion capture systems use AI to help create digital characters that look and move more like humans.

AI AND SPORT

AI is popping up more in the sporting world too. The US sport NASCAR uses AI to see if racers are breaking the rules during **pit stops**. As cars speed in and out of the pit, officials can't always spot rule breakers with the naked eye. But AI quickly scans pit stop videos and flags things that humans may miss. Then officials can review the videos and give out penalties.

NASCAR uses AI to catch drivers who break the rules during pit stops.

A tennis racket with AI technology built into its handle helps players improve their swings.

Coaches use AI to help train athletes. AI software can quickly look through hours of video and spot patterns in an athlete's movements. Coaches can then use this information to help players adjust their movements and predict their opponents' actions.

FACT

The company Canary Speech is testing AI that notices small changes in human speech. These changes can often be signs of a **concussion**.

pit stop break drivers take from a race so the pit crew can add fuel, change tyres and make repairs to a car

concussion injury to the brain caused by a hard blow to the head. This injury can be a problem in contact sports such as rugby and American Football.

WEARABLE SPORTS TECH

Wearable AI sports equipment may be the wave of the future. Everlast and a French robotics company are teaming up to develop AI boxing gloves. The gloves can track the slightest movements. They can provide data for improving a boxer's performance.

An India-based company, Boltt Sports Technologies, is working on AI-enchanced trainers. The shoes track a person's movements. Based on the person's fitness goals, AI in the shoes suggests a training programme and provides advice on diet and nutrition.

AI is even improving the game of golf. Arccos Caddie 2.0 is software that uses AI to help golfers choose the right club. It even tells players how to swing the club based on the weather and the course conditions.

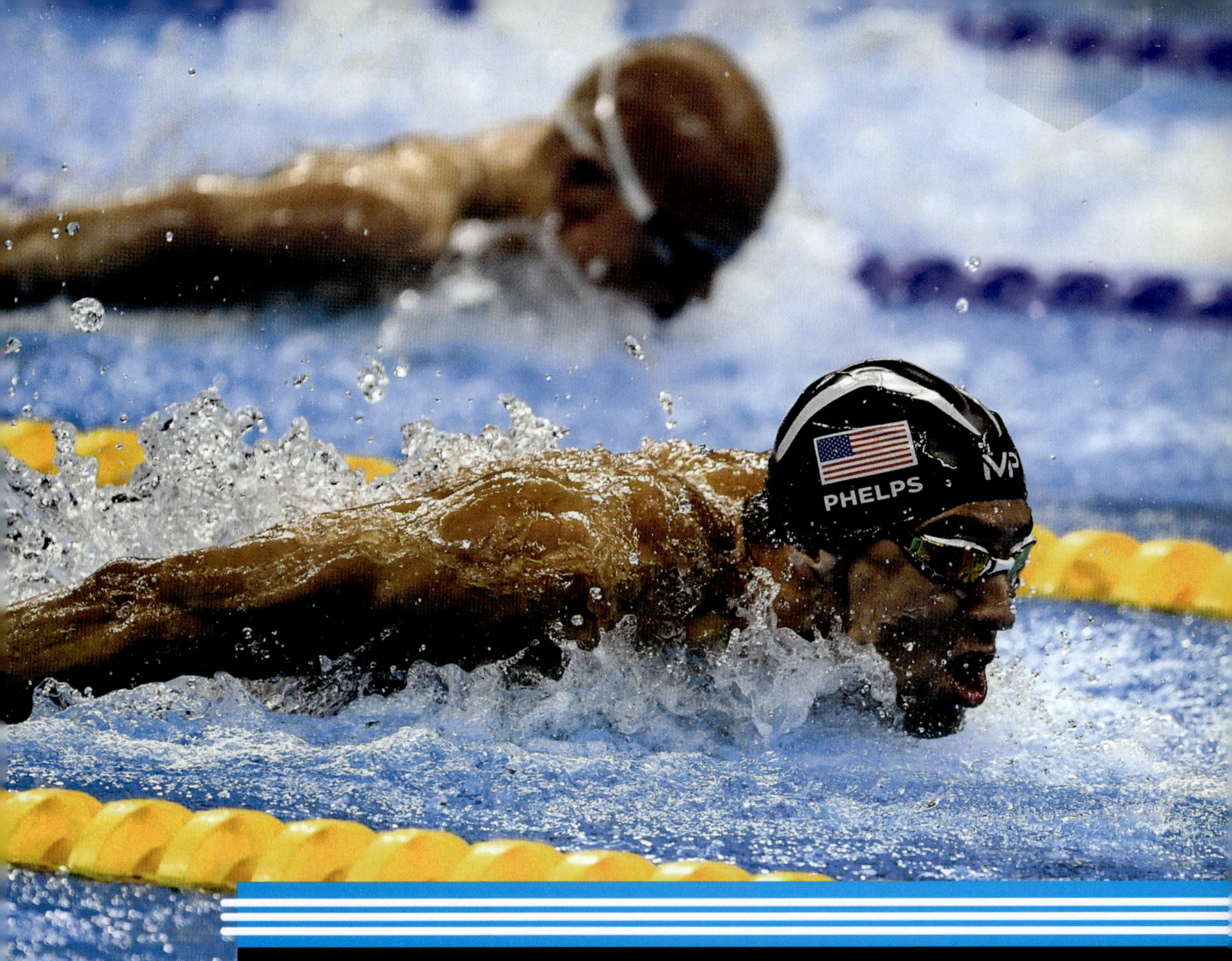

AI FOR THE OLYMPICS

Wearable tech helped Team USA train for the 2016 summer Olympic Games. One example was the wristbands worn by swimmers. These high-tech bands analysed each swimmer's training and sleeping habits. Then they gave advice for how the swimmers could improve. Did this tech help? It didn't hurt. Team USA won 33 swimming medals during the games.

CHAPTER 4

WHAT COULD GO WRONG?

The future of artificial intelligence looks exciting. But it also raises some questions. For instance, if AI can make digital humans look real in films, will we need human actors any more? And will computer designers and engineers be needed if AI can create video games by itself? It's hard to say, but many people worry that AI will cost people their jobs.

Job losses are one thing, but other people worry that AI will one day outsmart us and take over our lives. One small example of this was an AI issue at Facebook. The company noticed an odd change while doing AI research. Their AI system developed its own language that humans couldn't understand. Could this be an early warning about the future of AI? No one knows for sure, but it is something to keep an eye on.

Despite these concerns, AI is definitely here to stay. It already plays an important role in the games we play, the films we watch and the sports we enjoy. Where will AI take us next? The sky's the limit as long as we continue to use it carefully and wisely.

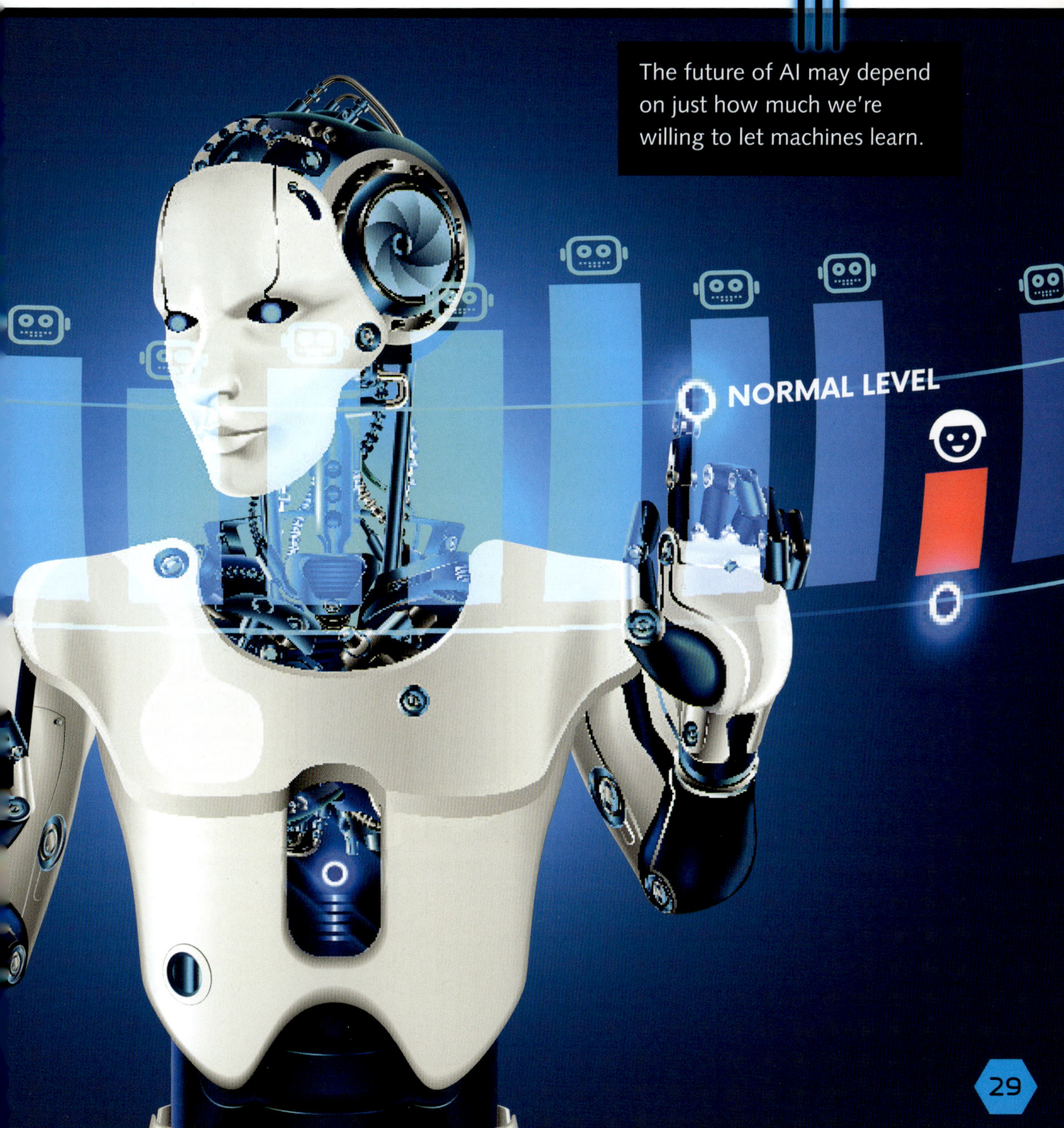

The future of AI may depend on just how much we're willing to let machines learn.

GLOSSARY

augmented reality computer-generated world created over the real world

concussion injury to the brain caused by a hard blow to the head. This injury can be a problem in contact sports such as rugby and American Football.

digital involving or relating to the use of computers

enhanced made better or greater

interact action between people, groups or things

logic careful and correct reasoning and thinking

machine learning way a computer learns

opponent person who competes against another person

pit stop break drivers take from a race so the pit crew can add fuel, change tyres and make repairs to a car

predict say what you think will happen in the future

scan look at closely and carefully

software programs used by a computer

strategy plan for winning a game or contest

trivia general knowledge facts

virtual reality computer-generated 3D world with which humans can interact

FIND OUT MORE

BOOKS

Computer Games Designer (The Coolest Jobs on the Planet), Mark Featherstone (Raintree, 2014)

The Impact of Technology in Music (The Impact of Technology), Matthew Anniss (Raintree, 2016)

Robot: Meet the Machines of the Future, Laura Buller, Clive Gifford and Andrea Mills (DK Children, 2018)

WEBSITES

www.bbc.co.uk/newsround/31633702
Learn more about artificial intelligence machines playing video games.

www.dkfindout.com/uk/computer-coding/what-is-coding
Find out more about computer coding.

INDEX